What people are saying  Let Animals Lead™ 21-Day Meditation Challenge

A beautifully simple way to add animals to your daily meditation practice. -Nuvea C.

I highly recommend this whether or not you ever are a Reiki practitioner. The difference it can make in how you relate to your world and animals and all living things around you is profound. -Sherry Z.

This challenge deepened my connection to a wide range of animals and provided a great structure in which to fully explore the energy of the Precepts. -Jenny M.

You will come out of this challenge with more compassion towards our animal and human companions. -Melissa G.

In 21 days, this meditation challenge had a profound effect on me and the peace and calm of my pride of kitties. It is something wonderful for everyone in the household, a blessing indeed. -Donna W.

I just finished Kathleen's 21-Day challenge, and it is amazing! For someone who's been meditating for a while, it's nice to come across a new way of connecting with animals that is so easy AND effective! The animals she has chosen are absolutely perfect! You'll love this! -Donna W.

I highly recommend this challenge to anyone who is looking to work on self-improvement and growth while incorporating the power and energy of our animal guides into their lives. Kathleen has presented a formula that makes it easy to embrace each animal's power and apply it to our own lives, helping to live a life according to the Reiki ideals. -Angie S.

This 21-Day Animal Reiki Meditation Challenge is a gentle way to connect with the energy of a range of different animals, while using the Reiki Precepts. This is a great way to get more familiar with the Reiki principles and to use them in your daily life. A must for anyone interested in Reiki and people who want to deepen their connection with animals. -Colleen M.

An easy-to-do challenge which also provide useful keys to connect deeply with the energy of animals, bring it into our daily life, and provide a great shift in consciousness. -Valeria P.

Let Animals Lead™ 21-Day Meditation Challenge

heal your life with the help of animals

Text Copyright © 2018 Kathleen Prasad. All rights reserved. No part of this publication may be reproduced, stored in a retrieval system, or transmitted in any form or by any means without the prior written permission of Ms. Prasad, nor be otherwise circulated in any form of binding or cover other than that in which it is published.

Published in the United States by Animal Reiki Source

ISBN- 978-0-9983580-2-4

Production: Leah D'Ambrosio

Interior photographs: ©Lexie Cataldo | www.InJoyPhotography.com, ©Jenny Loya and Adobe Stock.

Original animal artwork: Indigo Prasad

Cover art: ©Yvonne Cathcart | www.yvonnecathcart.com

DISCLAIMER: The suggestions in this manual are not intended as a substitute for professional veterinary care. Reiki sessions are given for the purpose of stress reduction and relaxation to promote healing. Reiki is not a substitute for medical diagnosis and treatment. Reiki practitioners do not diagnose conditions nor do they prescribe, perform medical treatment, nor interfere with the treatment of a licensed medical professional. It is recommended that animals be taken to a licensed veterinarian or licensed health care professional for any ailment they have.

Introduction and Description

Do you believe it is possible to change your life in 21 days? If you've joined Kathleen in any of her on-site workshops, you already understand the incredible power of the Animal Reiki journey and you're ready for more. If this will be your first time connecting with animals through Reiki meditation, get ready to discover the untapped potential that animals can awaken within you, and to open your heart and mind to loving-kindness, extraordinary bliss, and the balanced life of your dreams!

This is a course in empowerment. Meditating with the animals can help you let go of the things that are holding you back from finding your true happiness in life. The animals can help you uncover your inner healing potential. This course will nurture qualities within you that will bring success in every part of your life. At the end of this course, if you find yourself going back into anger and worry, you can repeat the course. Remember, the path of healing is a lifelong journey of peeling back the layers that cover up our inner light. The key is mindfulness through practice, practice, practice. The more we notice when we are out of balance, the easier it is to find our way back to true healing. Get ready to receive the joyful gifts of abundant healing; the animals will show you the way!

Directions for This Course

Daily Practice

Each day, for the next 21 days, I'd like you to begin and end each day by reciting the Five Reiki Precepts three times:

> For today only:
> Do not anger
> Do not worry
> Be humble, be grateful
> Be honest in your work
> Be compassionate to yourself and others

In addition, set aside at least five minutes of time each day to go over the day's animal meditation. Each day will also focus on a specific Reiki precept. Find a quiet space to sit, stand, or walk while reading over the day's information and contemplating the animal, the precept, and the affirmation.

Most importantly, keep the animal and affirmation as your mantra for the day, repeating it to yourself as you go through your normal activities. When you find yourself in a challenging moment, stop and take several hara breaths (description in next section) while focusing your mind and heart on the animal and affirmation.

Take time to reflect on how the animals, Reiki Precepts, affirmations, and breathing exercises helped to keep you balanced and peaceful through the day.

Focusing on the wisdom of animals can help bring peace and balance to our own lives, but meditating with the animals you share your life with is also a fun way to share the peaceful space we create! Be creative and find ways to include your animals in this meditation challenge. You'll be amazed at the peaceful, loving responses you'll get!

Spending time with our animals while we are meditating can help us develop our own sensitivities. Animals are wonderful models for us since they authentically embody so many spiritual qualities throughout their lives and even as they face death. Sharing meditation with animals can help guide us toward being better people and creating a healthier planet, because peace always starts inside of us before it can spread out to others.

Following are the three great ways to meditate with your animals during this course:

1) Sitting meditation. For this type of meditation, where you are sitting still with your eyes open and/or closed (as you prefer), you may want to purchase a meditation bench. It is also great to create a sacred, quiet space in your home where you can go and sit, and invite your animals to join you.

2) Standing meditation. For this meditation, find a peaceful place in nature (or with your horse or other animal nearby) to stand and connect deeply with the earth. You will find the natural elements naturally nurture the quiet space inside of you.

3) Walking meditation. For this meditation, find a place to walk that is quiet so that you can focus on the nature around you. If you are walking your dog, imagine you are connected heart to heart, rather than through the leash. While you are practicing this meditation, allow yourself to embrace nature all around you.

With the help of the animals in this course and the animals we live with, we can transform any stressful situation into a peaceful one. In so doing, we can see a wonderful transformation in the animals around us too, who are so sensitive and aware of our inner states of mind and heart.

The Hara Breath

Get in a comfortable position, spine nice and straight, and relax shoulders and arms. If you are sitting, hands are in your lap, palms up or down. If you are standing or walking, hands should be relaxed at the sides. Take a deep, cleansing breath, and let it out slowly. See the stresses of the day release with each exhale. Breathe in and exhale slowly a few times, focusing on your breath. Feel yourself letting go of all your concerns from the day as your breathe.

Bring your focus to your hara. The hara is your center, where the sacral chakra is, two or three finger-widths below the belly button. This is your grounding, your connection to earth. Imagine this center as a beautiful sphere of light in the center of your physical being, shining out a beautiful healing light in all directions.

Now focus on your breath. Breathe in through your nose, filling your whole body with healing light, all the way down to your hara. On the out breath, expand this light outward, through your skin, out into your aura, out into the room, out into the universe—as if you are filling a balloon with light. Do at least 10 of these hara breaths at your own pace each time you practice. With practice, you can spend 20 to 30 minutes doing the hara breathing.

Let Animals Lead™ 21-Day Meditation Challenge

Days 1-4
Do not anger.

Each of the animals and affirmations in this section will help you contemplate the healing gifts we receive when we let go of anger.

Directions for Each Day

Meditate

You may meditate sitting, standing, or walking. Begin by taking 10 hara breaths. Set your intent to invite the energy of the animal into the meditation to help you embody the animal's wisdom throughout the day.

Repeat the day's affirmation three times. Then focus on the hara breathing with your whole heart and mind—for five minutes, or as long as you like. When you are ready to finish, repeat the affirmation three times again. Thank the animal for sharing his wisdom with you.

Throughout Your Day

Visualize the animal with you throughout your day. When you face a difficult moment, connect with the animal, repeat the affirmation, and do some hara breaths to help bring you back into balance.

Notes

I stay centered within myself, and respond to all situations in a balanced way.

Let Animals Lead™ 21-Day Meditation Challenge

Day 1

Affirmation:

I stay centered within myself, and respond to all situations in a balanced way.

Bear energy is about grounding and strength. Bear radiates strength through heart connections. When we are truly grounded, the emotion of anger cannot knock us over. We can allow it to pass through us like wind through the branches of a tree. As anger loses its power over us, our hearts can truly shine.

I am at peace with all living beings.

Day 2

Affirmation:

I am at peace with all living beings.

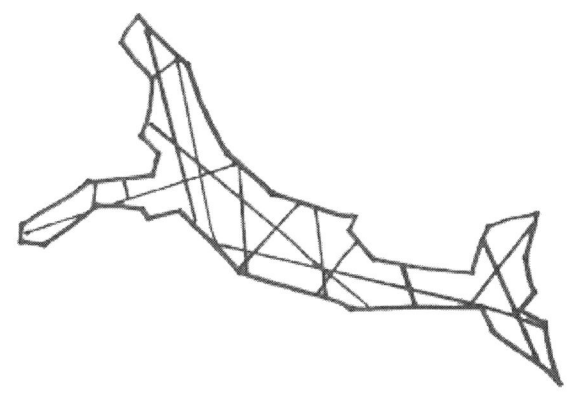

Whale energy is about peace and understanding. Whale helps us awaken our inner peace through remembering our connection to the whole. Anger keeps us separated from our inner wisdom and disconnects us from our relationships to others. As we let go of our anger, a deep inner peace can radiate out from us and help us to find harmony in all aspects of our lives.

I empower myself by listening to my inner voice.

Let Animals Lead™ 21-Day Meditation Challenge

Day 3

Affirmation:

I empower myself by listening to my inner voice.

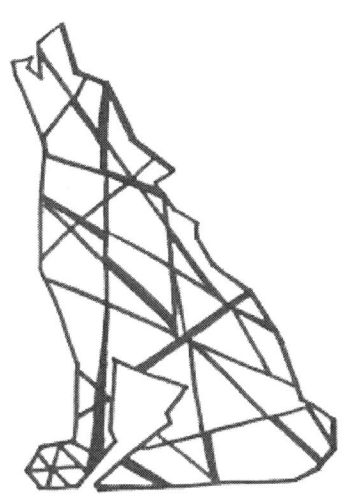

Wolf energy is about finding our inner power by tuning into our intuition. Anger silences the voice within, but wolf can help us to rebalance ourselves by remembering our inner wisdom. Listen to the quiet voice within your heart, and anger will lose its power.

Patience is my strength and my guide.

Day 4

Affirmation:

Patience is my strength and my guide.

Cougar energy helps us remember that there is great power in patience. Anger is an impulsive and draining energy, but cougar can help us empower ourselves and find clarity again through inner stillness. Be kind and patient with yourself; it is never too late to start again by just breathing.

Let Animals Lead™ 21-Day Meditation Challenge

Days 5-9

Do not worry.

Each of the animals and affirmations in this section will help you contemplate the healing gifts we receive when we let go of worry.

Directions for Each Day

Meditate

You may meditate sitting, standing, or walking. Begin by taking 10 hara breaths. Set your intent to invite the energy of the animal into the meditation to help you embody the animal's wisdom throughout the day.

Repeat the day's affirmation three times. Then focus on the hara breathing with your whole heart and mind—for five minutes, or as long as you like. When you are ready to finish, repeat the affirmation three times again. Thank the animal for sharing his wisdom with you.

Throughout Your Day

Visualize the animal with you throughout your day. When you face a difficult moment, connect with the animal, repeat the affirmation, and do some hara breaths to help bring you back into balance.

Notes

I am filled with courage and wisdom.

Day 5

Affirmation:

I am filled with courage and wisdom.

Lion energy helps us remember that each us of has the power to create our own world. When we face our fears with the ferocity of lion, worry loses its power and we can remember how strong we really are.

Day 6

Affirmation:

Each day I am closer to achieving my dreams.

Tiger energy helps us remember the power of determination. When we do not allow our worries to distract us, we are sure to attain our goals! Tiger helps us persevere, even through difficulties.

I find positive ways to overcome obstacles.

Day 7

Affirmation:

I find positive ways to overcome obstacles.

Ram energy helps us remember our inner courage. Rams easily navigate terrain that would cause others to be afraid or give up; they can help us find our courage to do the same. When we connect with the ram, we can uncover our inner boldness and positivity, allowing us to overcome any obstacles that come our way.

I embrace change.

Day 8

Affirmation:

I embrace change.

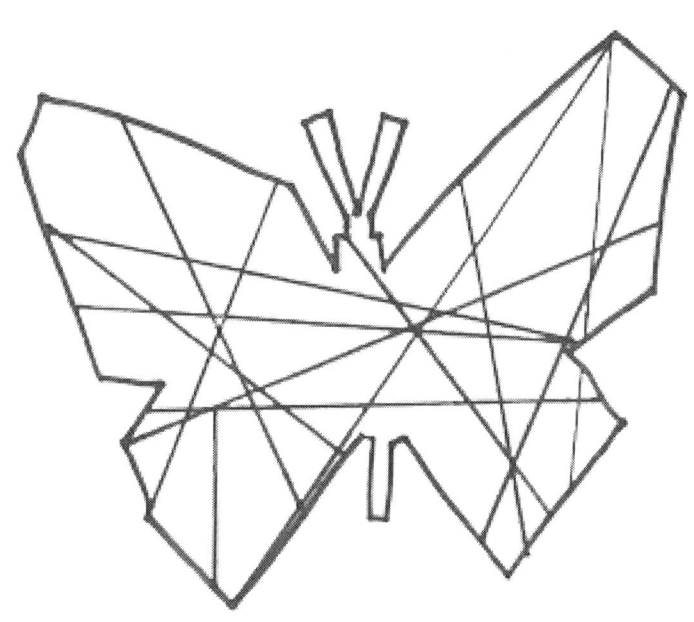

Butterfly energy helps us remember to be brave when our lives are in flux. When we let go of our fear the way a butterfly lets go of the cocoon, we can see the opportunities and blessings that lie ahead of us in times of change. Butterfly helps us become more welcoming of change and to thrive through uncertain times.

I give myself permission to let go of anger and worry.

Day 9

Affirmation:

I give myself permission to let go of anger and worry.

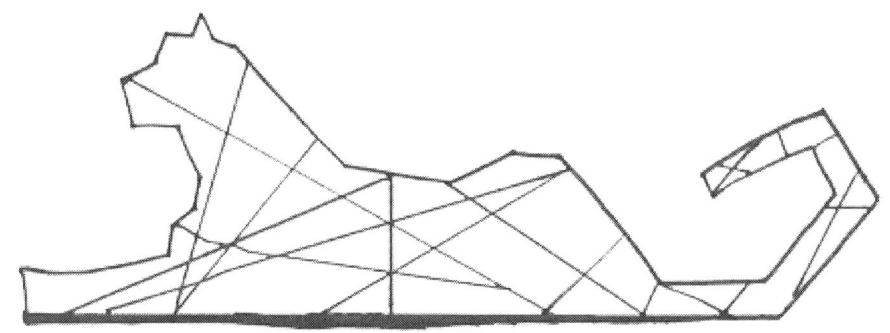

Black Leopard energy helps us to free ourselves of the bonds and cages that we build around us through our anger and worry. Rediscovering the free nature of our inner spirit, we realize that we can accomplish anything! In this way, black leopard helps us find the courage to let go and be free of old patterns so that we can reach our full potential.

Let Animals Lead™ 21-Day Meditation Challenge

Days 10-13

Be humble, be grateful.

Each of the animals and affirmations in this section will help you contemplate the healing gifts we receive when we remember to be humble and grateful.

Directions for Each Day

Meditate

You may meditate sitting, standing, or walking. Begin by taking 10 hara breaths. Set your intent to invite the energy of the animal into the meditation to help you embody the animal's wisdom throughout the day.

Repeat the day's affirmation three times. Then focus on the hara breathing with your whole heart and mind—for five minutes, or as long as you like. When you are ready to finish, repeat the affirmation three times again. Thank the animal for sharing his wisdom with you.

Throughout Your Day

Visualize the animal with you throughout your day. When you face a difficult moment, connect with the animal, repeat the affirmation, and do some hara breaths to help bring you back into balance.

Notes

I take responsibility for my own healing path, but I know to ask for help when I need it.

Day 10

Affirmation:

I take responsibility for my own healing path, but I know to ask for help when I need it.

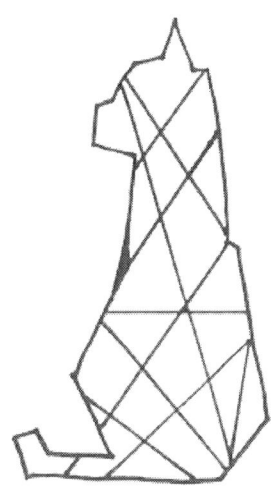

Cat energy helps us learn to balance independence with being able to accept assistance from others. It's important to be able to take responsibility for our own healing journey; but at the same time, a wise person knows when to ask for help. Cat helps us empower ourselves in a balanced and healthy way, from a place of gratitude for the support that others bring us.

I take time for self-healing and begin each day anew.

Day 11

Affirmation:

I take time for self-healing and begin each day anew.

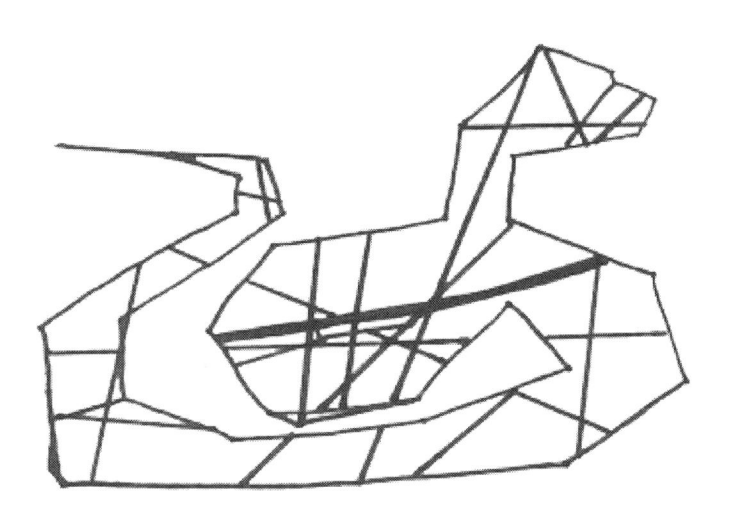

Snake energy helps us harness the power of renewal that daily self-healing can give us. Snake helps us connect with an ancient part of ourselves that can access deep healing, even in the most difficult times. Even the deepest suffering can be transformed into healing through the energy of snake. In this way we learn to be grateful for the lessons our struggles teach us.

Being flexible helps me strengthen and maintain life's balance.

Day 12

Affirmation:

Being flexible helps me strengthen and maintain life's balance.

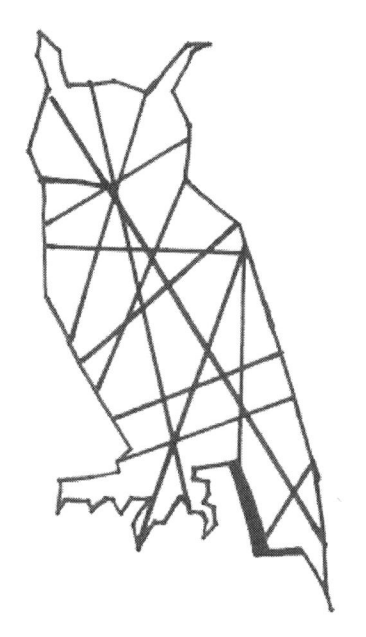

Owl energy helps us harness inner strength through flexibility. By connecting with owl's wisdom, you'll be guided through the illusion of ego to the path of true healing. Just like a willow tree that bends in the wind, owl will help you adapt to find the wise path in even the most challenging storms of change. Be grateful for these challenges, for they will build your inner strength.

My life is full of blessings.

Day 13

Affirmation:

My life is full of blessings.

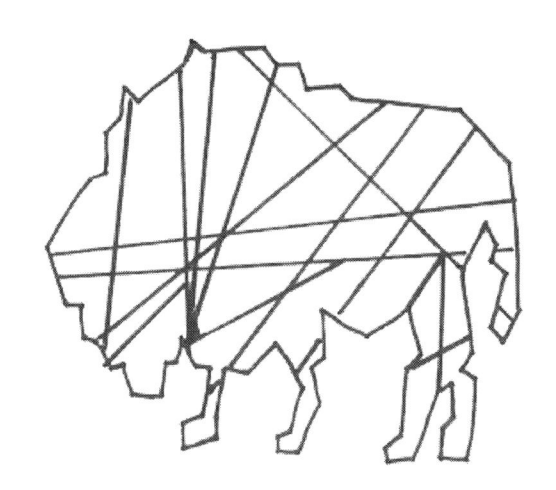

Buffalo energy brings to us the blessing of abundance. When we view situations from a space of humility and gratitude, healing and balance follow naturally. Buffalo helps us connect with our inner center and our connection to earth, so that even when life becomes difficult, we remember our blessings. When we are grounded, we can remember that this present moment is indeed a gift.

Days 14-17

Be honest in your work.

Each of the animals and affirmations in this section will help you contemplate the healing gifts we receive when we live with truth and authenticity.

Directions for Each Day

Meditate

You may meditate sitting, standing, or walking. Begin by taking 10 hara breaths. Set your intent to invite the energy of the animal into the meditation to help you embody the animal's wisdom throughout the day.

Repeat the day's affirmation three times. Then focus on the hara breathing with your whole heart and mind—for five minutes, or as long as you like. When you are ready to finish, repeat the affirmation three times again. Thank the animal for sharing his wisdom with you.

Throughout Your Day

Visualize the animal with you throughout your day. When you face a difficult moment, connect with the animal, repeat the affirmation, and do some hara breaths to help bring you back into balance.

Notes

My body, mind, and spirit are in perfect balance.

Day 14

Affirmation:

My body mind and spirit are in perfect balance.

Horse energy helps us harness the power of balance in all aspects of our being: physical, mental, emotional, and spiritual. Horse reminds us of our inner strength and will help you reconnect with your inner free spirit. The combination of inner strength and freedom will help you release thoughts and emotions that no longer serve you, so that you can move gracefully and easily past obstacles. This takes practice, and so we must work at this each day, each moment, with an honest heart.

In all that I do, my thoughts, words and actions align.

Day 15

Affirmation:

In all that I do, my thoughts, words and actions align.

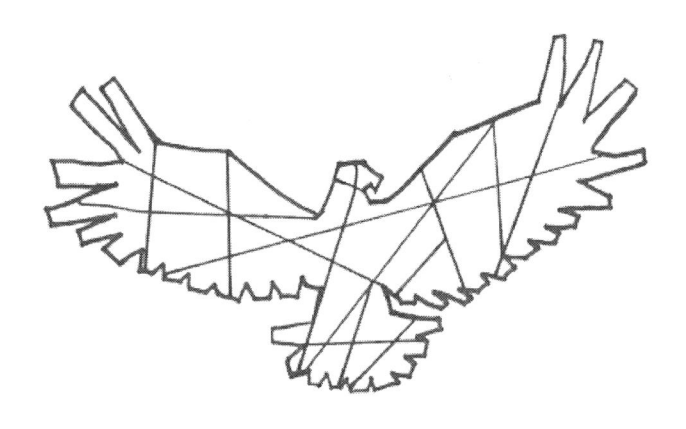

Eagle energy helps us harness the strength to take responsibility for our healing journey. Eagle helps open the doors to our higher vision and wisdom to see the best way forward. Eagle reminds us to be honest with ourselves about the way we give our power away through emotions such as anger and worry. When we center and harmonize our mind, body, and speech, we realize we are powerful and resilient, able to fly through the strongest winds of change or suffering.

I am connected to my body, mind and heart: the earth, sky and universe. We are all One.

Day 16

Affirmation:

I am connected to my body, mind and heart: the earth, sky and universe. We are all One.

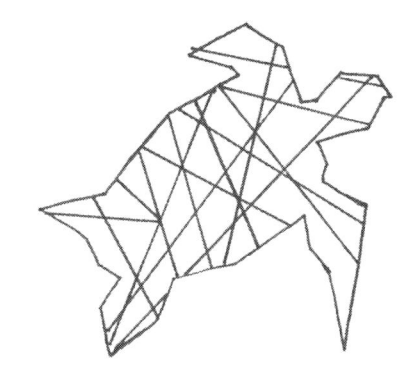

Turtle energy helps us choose the path of peace. Turtle reminds us to slow down and connect with the energy of Earth. When we do so, we access our most ancient wisdom, which is our inner essence. Turtle brings us closer to the truth of our connectedness in this universe; we are all One. When we are honest with ourselves, we know that when we hurt another, we also hurt ourselves. In turn, when we heal ourselves, this also supports the healing of others. This is as important a contemplation when sharing Reiki with animals as it is when sharing Reiki with humans.

I live in harmony with my heart's true purpose.

Day 17

Affirmation:

I live in harmony with my heart's true purpose.

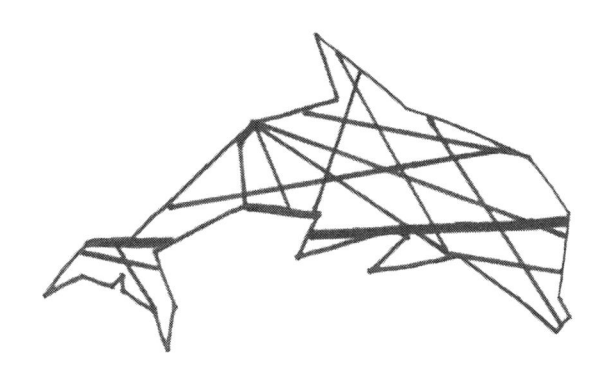

Dolphin energy helps us create harmony in the world around us. Dolphin helps us always communicate from the heart, which can help us harness the power of strong relationships and community. When we always connect heart to heart, it becomes much easier to reach out to others from an honest place, with love and care. In this way, dolphin opens the door to our inner truth and helps us to shine this light for others, spreading harmony wherever we go.

Days 18-21

Be compassionate to yourself and others.

Each of the animals and affirmations in this section will help you contemplate the healing gifts we receive when we find ways to show compassion to ourselves and others.

Directions for Each Day

Meditate

You may meditate sitting, standing, or walking. Begin by taking 10 hara breaths. Set your intent to invite the energy of the animal into the meditation to help you embody the animal's wisdom throughout the day.

Repeat the day's affirmation three times. Then focus on the hara breathing with your whole heart and mind—for five minutes, or as long as you like. When you are ready to finish, repeat the affirmation three times again. Thank the animal for sharing his wisdom with you.

Throughout Your Day

Visualize the animal with you throughout your day. When you face a difficult moment, connect with the animal, repeat the affirmation, and do some hara breaths to help bring you back into balance.

Let Animals Lead™ 21-Day Meditation Challenge

Notes

I honor other beings by listening not only with my ears, but also with my heart.

Day 18

Affirmation:

I honor other beings by listening not only with my ears, but also with my heart.

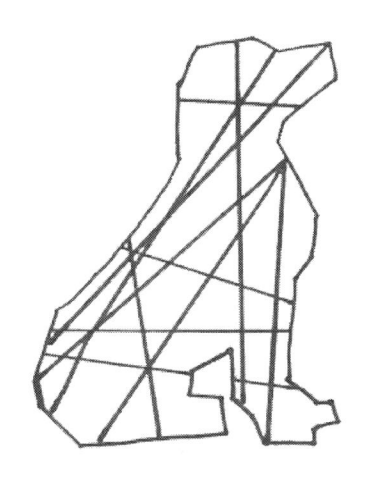

Dog energy helps us access the power of our inner heart and the unconditional love that resides there. Dog reminds us to be present in this moment and listen with our whole being to our loved ones. In this way we can show the ultimate respect and compassion to others. Dog also shows us that the healing power of presence doesn't have to be solemn; it can be playful and light-hearted.

I am loved and supported by my family, friends and community. I love and support them too.

Day 19

Affirmation:

I am loved and supported by my family, friends and community. I love and support them too.

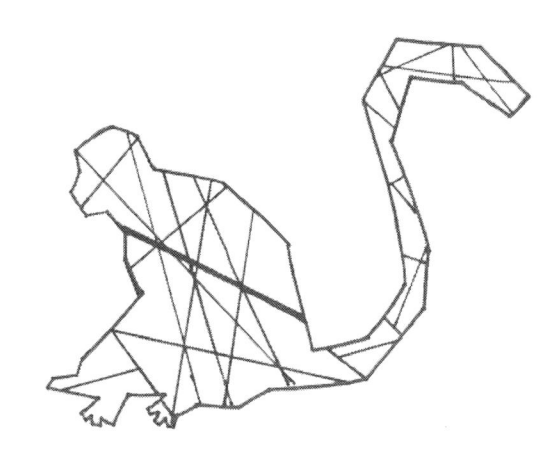

Monkey energy is quite lively and helps us build healthy community relationships. Monkey reminds us that compassion is not only about helping others, but also about being able to accept help when we need it. In a healthy community, there is a wonderful balance of giving and receiving, and there is great healing power in this kind of abundant flow. We need each other to live happy lives.

I practice compassion for my own healing and to help others.

Day 20

Affirmation:

I practice compassion for my own healing and to help others.

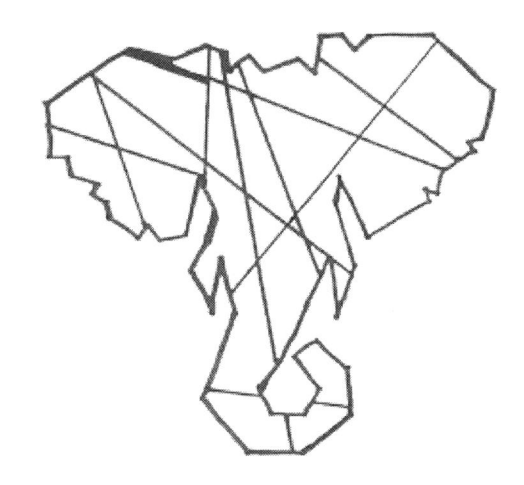

Elephant energy shows us the healing power of patience and temperance. Being compassionate doesn't mean we can't stand strong in our own truth; elephant can remind us how to stay true to our way and our being while staying kind and respectful of the ways of others. Elephant reminds us that the best way to create compassion in this world is to lead by example. Leave a powerful footprint in this world by spreading compassion wherever you go!

I choose to respond to all situations with kindness.

Day 21

Affirmation:

I choose to respond to all situations with kindness.

Deer energy helps us realize that our greatest strength lies in gentleness and kindness. Deer reminds us to face even the most challenging situations with grace, flexibility, and compassion. If we are vigilant, we will not give into our emotions of anger and fear. We can stay present and always respond with loving-kindness. Always stay mindful, always practice, and deer can show you the way to a kinder world.

Conclusion

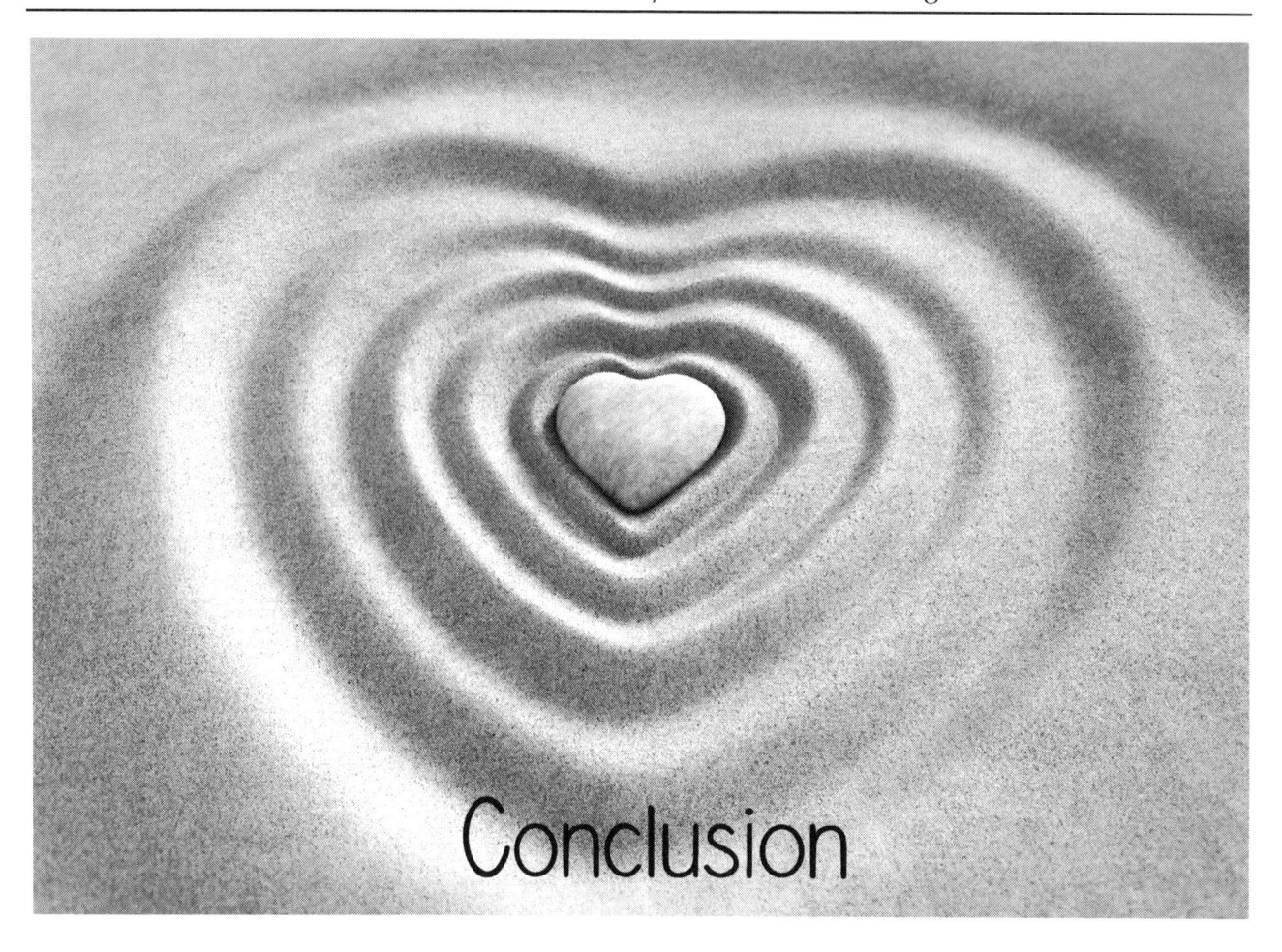

Now that the course is completed, it's time to reflect on how you have grown and changed with the help of the animals.

In the table below, reflect on what important lessons about yourself and healing the animals have taught you throughout this course.

Personal Challenges	How I Healed
Example: Before starting this course, I would frequently get angry and frustrated when driving in traffic.	I now feel peaceful when driving. I have compassion for others on the road. When I do start to feel angry, I bring in the energy of the bear and I start to feel grounded and calm again.

Personal Challenges	How I Healed

Personal Challenges

How I Healed

Personal Challenges

How I Healed

Final Thoughts

Congratulations on completing the *Let Animals Lead*™ 21-Day Meditation Challenge. I hope you enjoyed connecting with the many animal species in this program as much as I enjoyed creating it! My wish for you is that this brief introduction to the power of Reiki meditation with animals has opened new doors of mindful awareness and peaceful presence in your daily life. The Reiki Precepts are wonderful guides for living, and even more profound when we bring in the wisdom of animals as well! I encourage you to revisit the precept/animal/affirmation that resonates with you with each new situation or challenge you may face. You have the power to live a life of balance, no matter what challenges you face, and the animals can help you remember this!

May you be filled with peace and compassion, and may the animals light your way...

Kathleen Prasad

Animal Reiki Prayer for the World

By Kathleen Prasad

To all animals, domesticated and wild, you are in my heart ...

those used merely for food production
those who find themselves hunted
those who lose their lives in the name of science and research
those dwelling in zoos and wildlife parks
those lucky to be safe in loving homes
those rescued and waiting for their forever family in shelters
those blessed to find respite in sanctuaries
those who are healthy
those who are facing physical, emotional or spiritual challenges
those who are babies newly born on this earth
those in the prime of life, those winding down and those ready to cross the rainbow bridge....

May your body be comfortable, safe and well
May your mind be happy, peaceful and radiant like the sky
May your spirit be in harmony, balance and unity with the universe
May you be respected, cherished, liberated and free

And to all humans on this earth...

May you be embraced with wellbeing and harmony.
May you walk the path of grace, gentleness and compassion for all.
May your minds awaken in gratitude for the healing gifts of the animals
May your hearts radiate with the light of kindness.
May you be the voice for the voiceless, a lighthouse for the lost and a helping hand for the ailing.

May all beings live in the peace, harmony, love and compassion that is Reiki. May sharing the practice of Reiki with each other help us to remember our perfect inner light and healing potential.

Let's hold these words for a moment in our hearts and now send them out with blessings and love into the universe.

Be peace, be light, be love and be Reiki.

And as you travel the road of healing, may the animals light your way!

About the Author

Kathleen Prasad is founder of Animal Reiki Source and president of the Shelter Animal Reiki Association (SARA). A Reiki practitioner since 1998, Kathleen Prasad formed Animal Reiki Source to teach and share the healing benefits of Reiki for animals and their caregivers. Kathleen's teachings, based on traditional Japanese Reiki techniques and thousands of hours of Animal Reiki experience in the field, represent the world's first specialized, extensive and professional curriculum in animal Reiki.

In Kathleen's nonprofit SARA, volunteer members, guided by Kathleen's teachings, support animal rescue centers around the world. Kathleen has taught Animal Reiki to shelter staff, volunteers and animal lovers in locations around the world such as BrightHaven, Best Friends Animal Society, The San Francisco SPCA, Guide Dogs for the Blind, The CARE Foundation, The Elephant Sanctuary, Animal Haven, The Devoted Barn, Animal Protection Society and Remus Memorial Horse Sanctuary. Kathleen is the author of *Healing Virtues, Heart To Heart With Horses: The Equine Lover's Guide to Reiki, Everything Animal Reiki* and *Reiki for Dogs*.

Kathleen is the originator of the *Let Animals Lead*™ method of Animal Reiki. This method includes 6 pillars of practice:

1. It is founded upon traditional Japanese Reiki techniques and philosophy.
2. Animal Reiki is mindfulness meditation practiced "with" our animals, rather than an energy therapy done "to" them.
3. Meditation is taught as a state of mind with flexible physical forms.
4. Touch is used only when animals seek it out, and then only as a compassionate support.
5. Mental focus techniques develop an "All is Well" state of mind for the practitioner that sees the animal's perfection in this moment. Kathleen calls this seeing with your "Reiki eyes," in other words, seeing more deeply, with your heart.
6. This method acknowledges and honors each animal as a spiritual teacher and healer in his/her own right. Practitioners learn to listen and become receptive to their spiritual wisdom and healing gifts.

For more information, please visit: www.AnimalReikiSource.com or www.ShelterAnimalReikiAssociation.org.

Made in the USA
Lexington, KY
03 December 2018